Bus Ride…(s)

Scott Shaw

Buddha Rose Publications

Front Cover Painting by Scott Shaw

First Edition 1988
Second Edition 2011

ISBN 10: 1-877792-23-3
ISBN 13: 978-1-877792-23-6

10 9 8 7 6 5 4 3 2 1

Printed in the United States of America

Bus Ride...(s)

I took a bus ride one day...
(two day...s). I took it from my
Hermosa Beach apartment to
Hollywood. Hollywood, where my
vehicle...(s) had broken down and
repair was taking place. I took a
notebook along with me. These are
the words which I placed upon its
lines.

That was four year...(s) ago;
four year...(s) past.

One of the car...(s), it is
gone. The apartment, moved out
of, long ago. The L.A. bus, never
want to touch another. And life, it
does go on...

I am sitting here: L.A.,
summer day, the ocean roars
outside my window. The beach
crowds, I hear them too. And I, I
sit here, in all my perpetual
artistic frustration; alone.

(Don't desire to a poet, an artist, for it is not all that it is cracked up to be)...

I came upon this notebook, the bus ride...(s) notebook and decided to place these words to type on this day as they ocean waves crash, outside my window, and the beach crowds bath in the sun.

S.
88.19.8
Redondo Beach, California

Bus Ride

31 October 1984

Hermosa Beach,
Sixth and Hermosa,
to Hollywood
to pick-up my VW pickup.

1

sit here
well, stand here
swallow my pride
the bench is wet
can't sit down
wait for the bus
to arrive
the 42
to downtown

2

California
where everyone has a car

several...

I have several

California
where no one has friends
I join the club
I have to take the bus

3

hyper sensation
my stomach races
I wait
what time does the bus come?
how many an hour?
now 7:52 AM
I went to bed at 4:00 AM
after a session with the grape
I'm tired
I wait

4

I had a momentary fantasy once
not so long ago
of taking a day
of taking a bus
wherever I ended up
write the day
write the experience
etc., etc., etc...
I guess this
will have to do

5

clothing wore:
white adidas tennis shoes
from the ground up
grey, baggy
cuffed pants
green shirt
greyish tweed, small lapel
sport coat
Rolex watch
black sunglasses
my style

hair
parted on the side
long in back
long in front
hangs in my face
unshaven
four days now

the look
ah, the look

look of mind
my look of time
I am only
who I am

is that an
only statement?

6

a bus passes
the other way
does that mean that mine
is close at hand
maybe
maybe, I don't know

people in cars
they pass
do they realize
that I own two Porsche(s)

when I see a person at the bus stop
I just think,
a person on the bus stop
apparently no car

the obvious
is deceiving

7

out of the apartment
walks

the front apartment
the one behind me

a girl
a girl I have seen
and said, *"Hi,"* to
many times

Mexican girl, I think

in fact,
once while walking *The Strand*
on a Saturday night
me, with my main and current
L.A. babe
I saw her
she said, *"Hi."*
my main and current L.A. babe
got pissed

anyway...
16

she knows my cars
knows of me
our apartment buildings
are only an alley apart

interesting...
she sits
warms her car up
drives off
but she doesn't ask if I need a ride
I would have asked...

life
why a need for egotism
why the necessity
to develop humility

I see where
the roots
of egotism lie

8

I see the bus
in the distance
I put on my glasses
to see its number better
for two buses stop
stop at this bus stop

42
130

it comes
my bos
number 42
I get on

"How much to downtown with a transfer?"
"Sixty cents."
"Thank you."
"You're welcome."

9

on the bus ride
front/sideways seat
a bitchy looking rich girl

to the left
an older blue collar worker
and a hippie, redneck style

to the right
an impending old man
work shirt around his neck
various other people
younger and older
richer/poorer
the wise and the fools
workers
doers
the dysfunctional
the functionally insane
secretaries
like that one
that one over to my right
she is writing
as I am writing

I wonder if she is taking
a poetic journey, as well

and the others
more than not
more than low life
the lower life
of L.A.
the less fortunate
the etc...

is someone going
to sit next to me
will I then
be able to continue to write

the lady/the secretary
she sits on the isle
I, I sit by the window
she is not
inviting anyone to sit
next to her
but than
neither am I

20

10

Manhattan Beach Boulevard
Manhattan Beach Pier
the water grey
shore-pounder waves
the sky
grey to blue
Manhattan Beach

11

it is funny
not inviting people
to sit next to me
I am,
to use the description
of others,
a somewhat backward person
I am
perhaps,
more in my own words,
somewhat introverted

why
an only child's choice?
I don't know
I like friends
I like women
I must look
deeper into this

12

the bus drives
Highland Avenue
a boy waves
mid-block
expecting the bus to stop

the bus does not
the driver
a thirty-ish black bus driver
waves back
and drives on
as an old lady
sounds her disapproval

13

130
bus to Fullerton
Orange County
down Artesia
42
bus to downtown
Union Station

14

behind me
a man
sneezing, coughing
he finished
another man says,
"Bless you."
"Thank you."

personally,
I wish he would keep his germs
to himself

15

approaching people
the bus
begins to fill
still no one
sitting next to me
they chose the other seats
good
sitting next to me
would obviously inhibit
my writing

it is funny how the world
brings strange pressures
or perhaps
just how I deal with them

I feel somewhat of a knot
in my stomach
over the possibility
of someone sitting next to me
and hindering my writing

but all in the experiment
of riding the bus

16

once on the bus
it is so much nicer
than standing on the street
you move into the world
of people
of similar kind

bus-riders

known and looked at
known and looked down upon
seen by the car driving masses
known by the passer-bys
but here
they are of the similar kind

bus-riders
they are home

17

it's funny
I sit here
picking and choosing
the people who get on the bus
whether it would be okay
if this person or if that person
sat next to me

well, she's okay
no way, to that dude

maybe writing
will deter them
maybe my vibes
but the whole thing
takes away the peace

I must learn
in all situations
to flow
a little bit more

sit back
and watch

18

Paris, Tokyo, London
it is great to ride
public transportation

subways
everyone has a chance to meet
one another

it is nice

L.A. bus service
only low life
it's fucked
no satisfaction
no illusion
nothing at all

conquering and understanding
the local rapid transit

19

LAX stop point
a wetback
sits next to me
why not a beautiful woman
instead
anything but
a smelly wetback
thermos in hand
who is rappin'
Espanol
to his *compadre*
in the next seat over

20

El Mexicano
gets off
a few stops later
Westchester…

    what a judgmental person
    I am

    let all be
    as they be
    what they want to be
    you never know
    who you gain from

it's funny
late night at Fat Burger
a couple of nights ago
a Latina girl
early twenties
semi-babish
I mean I was interested
in a lusty sort of way

she worked there
and she was looking at me

how funny
what a space
I often come from
and how I view people
at times
so sexist
so judgmental
so hollow
it amazes even me

21

low life
ghetto lady
waiting for the bus
age, maybe twenty
a baby in her arms
a stroller in one hand
a cigarette in the other
tight jeans
tight tee shirt
can't she see

22

Santa Barbara Avenue
now,
Martin Luther King Jr. B.L.V.D.
drive past
the old house
my old house
maybe seventeen years now
since I lived there
G&J market
still across the street

PART II

There was another bus ride, another time. The same notebook in hand.

The reason...(s), the same. The purpose, the same. And, the intent, to make the moments of emptiness turn into something of suchness.

Bus Journal

Continued...

7 May 1985

now, 7:44 PM

on my way:
Hermosa, to downtown,
to Hollywood
to pickup my *'64 Porsche 356 SC*

23

the only time
I ride the bus in L.A.
seems to be concerning
my cars

tonight
as the spring sky darkens
as my ego
is shrinking
sitting
on a beach bus bench
I wait

just before I left
my Hermosa Beach apartment
my messy
my very messy
Hermosa Beach apartment
I find on the floor
a document
of foreign exchange

money exchange
in December

at the
Tokyo Hilton International

how I want to travel back
in many ways it is funny though
it seems
time has gone by so fast
what is it now
almost five months
since I was last in Japan
seems only a minute
and my life style
and condition
keeps me burned out
seeking a purpose
seeking a reason
trying to make
bus rides
which I don't wish to take
poetic

24

the bus comes
the bus stops
I get on
some pretty lady
sitting
I sit
on the right

the right
first time on the bus
usually, I choose the left

the lady gets off

25

Latin lady
talking to the bus driver
slurring her words
must have tipped a few back

"Everyone likes L.A.,
I think.
It's big
but there's little cities.
I like it.
I'm not depressed here."

L.A.
city of love
city of hate

I love it/I hate it

a black man
talks to the bus driver

"I'm going to buy a car,
a VW Rabbit.
That's my dream car."

small dream
I think

L.A.
a city of big dreams
everyone,
well almost everyone
want to be someone
or someone else

the bus driver asks the lady,
*"When are you going home
to visit Mexico?"*

"At Christmas,"
she says
*"I talk my parents
a lot
Talk, on the telephone."*

*"Did you tell them
that you met
a nice bus driver
named Charlie?"*

(laughter)

meeting
meeting who
meeting what

life and its pursuits
lives with no vision
no purpose
seeking only lust
seeking only money
fame
fortune
to pay the rent
not truth

*"How is your immigration
coming,"*
Charlie asks

*"Well, my visa expires
next month but I want to
stay."*

*"You can marry a nice
bus driver, can't you?"*

"Yes."

(laughter)

marriage to marriage
marrying what?
a vision
a dream
true love
no
only a person
a black bus driver
named Charlie

the story of L.A.
desires
cars
illegal immigration
and I ride the bus

26

Latin lady
looks at me
out of the corner of her eye

I look away
all so casually

her arm is stretched out
on the seat
I see her breasts
gently bounce
I see her ornamented bra
through the veil
of her soft white shirt

could there be interest in me?

no chance

earrings; many
hair long
1940's suit
and I'm not a black bus driver

just me
riding the L.A. bus
L.A. bus of desireless desire
going to nowhere
via downtown L.A.
to pick up my Porsche

    I wonder
    what the young black man
    who desires
    a VW Rabbit
    would do
    with two Porsches
    an MG
    a '66 Mustang
    and a VW pickup truck

    for that matter
    what would I do with them
    I mean
    I have them
    and what do I do
    I ride the bus
    to pick them up

27

bus driver
gives the expiring visa lady
his telephone number
tells her when to call

can't blame a soul boy for trying

28

fat slob
sit
in the seat
in front of me
well,
let's say he falls
into the seat

he smells
life smells
the bus
only perpetuates it

as we drive
into the inner city

29

Charlie,
the bus driver
is laying the rap
to this young boy
who is complaining
about losing his text book

"You know,
it's that devil that causes
all those problems.
It's his work,
so you have to work harder
to make that devil look bad."

the rap
so says, Charlie
the bus driver

30

downtown L.A.
at night
I arrive here
it is dark
it feels like
Hong Kong, Singapore, Berlin
I hear Chinese being spoken
I see Blacks and Latinos
I even watch a fag
trying to pickup
on a young Chinese bootie boy

drag queens
climb on the bus to Hollywood
cops
bust a bum

the streets
these are the real streets

the street
of the night

31

I ride the new bus/the next bus
downtown L.A. to Hollywood
through the window
I see an old man
with very long hair
is he making a statement
or is he just weird

the bus turns
drives down Sunset B.L.V.D.
it stops
at the English school on Sunset
a lot of ladies getting on
I would be lying
if I said
I did not look with desire
at a few of them

(the chase)

now, I know
I could play the game better
look conservative
look conversive
52

and attract a lot more
but I like
what I like
and I wonder
where does
making a statement end
and weird begin
I guess it begins
in the eyes of others

so, to the chase
so, to the dance
and here it is to being

who and what
be who you really want to be
no matter how alone
it leaves you
or how weird
it makes you appear

32

life to nowhere
ride it on the bus
say a prayer
and you find
what you find